IT'S NEVER TOO EARLY

Sponsored by
MLC LIMITED

Published in association with the Association of
Superannuation Funds of Australia Limited

CONTENTS

Introduction	vii
1 What is super?	**1**
What is the Superannuation Guarantee Charge?	2
How does super work?	3
What types of fund are there?	5
Who looks after my money?	6
What happens to my money?	8
2 Why do I need super?	**11**
Should I put some of my own money into super?	13
Wouldn't I be better off leaving my money in the bank?	15
What about investing it myself?	16
Why shouldn't I spend my money now?	17
3 How do I look after my super?	**19**
How much do I have to pay in fees?	20
How do I find out what fees I have to pay?	23
What about taxes?	23
What do I do if I leave my job?	25
Can I still add to my super if I leave the workforce?	27
What do I do if I've lost my super?	29
Do I have a say in how my super is invested?	30

Can I choose which super fund my money
    goes into? 32
How do relationships affect my super? 32
What do I do if I'm self-employed? 33
Is my money safe in super? 35
What do I do if I have a problem with my
    super? 37

4 When do I get my money? **40**
How is it paid to me? 45
Will I get the pension? 47

Interviews **49**

Response **68**

For more information **75**

Glossary **77**

INTRODUCTION

If you are under the age of thirty, it's a fair bet that you haven't given much thought to super. 'Why bother to put money away for my future when there's so much I can do with it now?', you might ask. If you gave people the option of taking their super as part of their wages, it wouldn't be hard to guess what most would say. The prospect of retiring some time in the next millennium is too far off to even think about, let alone have it affect your spending habits.

But due to the initiatives of the government and unions, super has undergone substantial changes in recent years which affect us all. With the 'baby boomer' generation rapidly approaching retirement, concern that the level of retirement savings was too low led to the introduction of compulsory super by the Commonwealth government from 1 July 1992. This followed the introduction of super through most industrial awards.

Put simply, this means that, depending on the size of the company payroll and individual earnings, a contribution which equals a certain percentage of an employee's salary must be paid into a super fund by the employer, if it is not being paid already. This percentage will increase in coming years until 2002 when employers will be paying 9 per cent of their employees' salary into super. In addition, the federal government announced plans in the 1995 Budget to phase in compulsory employee contributions from 1 July 1997 until the employee is paying 3 per cent of take-home pay in the year 2000. These employee contributions will be matched by the government dollar for dollar (subject to a means test). As a result, in 2002 nearly all workers will have an equivalent of at least 15 per cent of their pay contributed towards their super. Nine per cent will be paid by the employer, 3 per cent by the government and 3 per cent will come out of the employee's after-tax pay. This money will be invested in the employee's name in order to provide an income after retirement.

Put even more simply it means that if an employer pays you at least $450 in a month, you are already saving for retirement.

Scary thought?

It needn't be. While super can be confusing for those of us who aren't lawyers, accountants or actuaries, if you are aware of what you are entitled to and the procedures to monitor and manage your account, the subject of super will be a lot less intimidating. In addition, having a well established super plan will be an advantage when the time comes to consider your retirement more seriously.

One of the big pluses of super is that it gives you the chance to invest in the economy, help it to prosper, and, in turn, gain from its growth. Currently, Australians have invested around $187 billion in super plans and 85 per cent of that is invested on our shores. It beats the hell out of borrowing money from overseas.

For most, the only exposure to super has been completing a form when starting a job or receiving an annual statement from a fund administrator. Since the money doesn't physically come out of the pocket, and it can't be withdrawn as if it were in a bank account, it's easily neglected. But it's important to remember that even though access is restricted, this money is *yours* and it's worth your while to take an interest in what happens to it because eventually you will be putting it in your pocket.

For others, super is not just a confusing jumble of paper work and financial bureaucracy, but a path to financial security. However, many who think super is a good idea in principle are put off by the complexities of the industry, and are suspicious their money will not grow.

The intention of this book is not to make you rush off to your nearest insurance agent and have them relieve you of all your spare cash. Instead, its goal is to explain clearly and simply what super is about and how it affects young people. Hopefully, it will give you a better idea of why the federal government is promoting super as a comprehensive savings strategy and how it can work for you, so that any choice you make will be an informed one.

The book is divided into two parts. The first part is an explanation of how super funds work. It is designed to answer some of the questions most commonly asked. The second part is a series of interviews with young people along with short answers to the questions they raise.

CHAPTER 1
WHAT IS SUPER?

Superannuation is a long-term saving plan designed to provide income during retirement. In most cases savings are placed in accounts administered by a super fund which will pay you an amount, known as a benefit, when you retire. But as most of you are probably aware, there is a lot more to super than just two sentences.

For most young people retirement will not come for another 40 years or so. In the meantime a whole variety of work opportunities will present themselves. Right now some of you may be starting TAFE or university courses, while others are just finishing. You might be entering the workforce for the first time, in a job that could prove to be the start of a life-long career or could last only six months. Others are unemployed and looking for a fresh start.

As this generation advances towards the lawn bowling years, the one certain thing is uncertainty. Our working lives are more likely than not to take numerous twists and turns, many of them totally unpredictable. While it might have been typical 20 years ago for your average retiree to be a 60-year-old male who worked with the same company since the age of 16, in the future a 65-year-old woman who has worked at 8 different jobs, made 3 career changes and took time off from the workforce to have 2 children, may be more typical.

In keeping with the changing nature of work, super is changing too. In years gone by it was better known as the

2 IT'S NEVER TOO EARLY

'golden handshake': a lump sum given to an employee for years of faithful service with only 5 cents in the dollar subject to tax. As the name suggests, it was a bonus which rewarded loyal management staff as well as providing an avenue for companies to reduce their tax. The majority of those not in the position to receive this privilege had no retirement fund. However, due to the introduction of compulsory super, around 70 per cent of part-time workers and 90 per cent of those working full time are now members of a super fund.

WHAT IS THE SUPERANNUATION GUARANTEE CHARGE?

EMPLOYER CONTRIBUTIONS

The Superannuation Guarantee Charge requires an employer to make super contributions on behalf of any employee earning at least $450 a month. If the employer doesn't pay the super then the employer must pay the Tax Office a charge equal to what the employee should have been paid in the first place, along with interest and penalties.

For 1995/96 the scale of payment is 5 per cent of earnings if you work in a company which spends less than 1 million on wages, and 6 per cent if it spends more than 1 million. This will be increased gradually until your employer is contributing 9 per cent of your pay in 2002, no matter what the size of the company payroll. Nine per cent might not seem like a fortune, but in today's terms if you're earning a salary of $400 a week your employer will contribute $36 to your super. Over a year that amounts to $1872. On top of this there is the federal government's intention to increase this amount to 15 per cent by matching your own contributions, of 3 per cent of your pay, dollar for dollar (subject to a means test). This would bring the annual super contribution up to $3120 for those on $400 a week, which is anything but chicken feed.

When starting a job it's likely that your employer will tell you what super you'll get, whether it is what the Superannuation Guarantee provides for, or an amount larger than that. Your fund will also inform you through an annual statement of your super account. Many of you will be working in areas that are covered by awards which extend to super. Most awards require employers to pay the equivalent of the Superannuation Guarantee; however, some may differ. In this case, the employer is required to pay whatever is greater.

HOW DOES SUPER WORK?

The money is paid into a super fund, which is an investment scheme designed to accept your super contributions and invest them so as to increase their value before they're paid to you when you retire.

There are two basic styles adopted by super funds to determine your benefit (the amount of money you get when your super is paid out): accumulation and defined benefit.

- **Accumulation**
  Money is paid into the super fund, usually a fixed percentage of your wage, and earns interest through investment until it is paid out as a benefit when you retire. The amount you receive is what's left—minus tax and administration costs—of the contributions made to your account, plus the interest these contributions have earned.

- **Defined benefit**
  Defined benefit funds differ from accumulation funds in the manner in which the member receives their benefit. The benefit you will receive as a member of such a fund is set at a definite figure whereas the benefit you would receive from an accumulation style fund depends on what's added to your account and what's taken out. A common method employed by defined benefit style funds is to calculate your benefit according to your final salary and how long you have been a member. For example, 4 times the salary you earn just prior to retirement after 40 years in the fund, 3 times after 30 years and so on. The employee often contributes a set percentage of pay and the employer makes up the rest. In good years employer contributions may be small but when the returns are not so good then your employer is forced to contribute more.

More than likely you belong to an accumulation style super fund. With the introduction of compulsory super payments, many employers have had to establish, or

WHAT IS SUPER?

broaden, their employees' super funds. From the employer's point of view, accumulation style funds are generally simpler to operate and your employer does not have to carry the risk of poor investment as is the case with defined benefit funds.

Since most of us are members of accumulation super funds, we will concentrate on this style in particular.

WHAT TYPES OF FUND ARE THERE?

There are basically four types of fund:

- **Company funds**
  These are funds established by your employer to accept contributions on your behalf, whether they are from you or your boss. Such funds are usually only offered by large companies which because of their size can afford to operate a fund exclusively for their employees' benefit.

- **Industry funds**
  Industry funds are developed by unions and/or employer groups associated with a particular industry and usually work on the accumulation style. Some of these funds have been around for a while and have built up large pools of assets. If you work in the building, hospitality or retail industries, for example, it's a good chance you belong to an industry fund.

- **Public sector funds**
  Reserved for government employees, public sector funds are set up by an act of parliament and as a result are heavily regulated as they must also comply with some of the general legislation for the industry.

- **Public offer funds**
  These funds are the odd ones out as they are not linked to the occupation of their members. They are set up by banks, insurance companies and the like, and are open to anyone who wants to join. They provide super for employees of a firm without its own fund, the self-employed or those who wish to have a personal super fund. Different public offer funds vary significantly in fee costs and investment style.

WHO LOOKS AFTER MY MONEY?

There are basically three groups of people who have something to do with your money in super:

Trustees

Super funds are established through a trust deed (a legal document which, for want of a better description, is the rule book governing the operation of the fund) or in the case of public sector funds by an act of parliament. The people who ensure the fund operates according to the trust deed are called trustees. The trustees are selected according to the terms of the trust deed. From 1 July 1995 every fund that has more than 5 members must have half the positions on the board of trustees appointed to represent the members' interests and half to represent the employer's. Funds with fewer than 50 members may, if the majority of members agree, decide to appoint an independent corporate trustee approved by the government. Public offer funds must have an independent corporate trustee approved by the government.

WHAT IS SUPER?

Trustees have certain obligations that are outlined in legislation and the trust deed. They are the people ultimately responsible for your money, and above all else trustees *must* act in the best interests of the fund members (i.e. you and me). To do this they may have to delegate certain duties if others are able to perform them better.

Administrators

A fund administrator is a person or company which handles the day to day affairs of the fund. For example, keeping records, providing information to members and calculating benefits. Larger superannuation funds will have people employed to carry out these tasks; however, in other cases a separate company which specialises in fund administration may have been employed by the trustees to dot the Is and cross the Ts in your super.

Investment managers

Because investing money is a tricky game, people who are skilled in this area are appointed by the trustees. Investment managers can be individuals or companies and they buy assets with your money according to a broad investment strategy set out by the trustees. For example, the trustees may decide that a certain percentage of the money should be invested in property, so it is then up to the investment managers to decide which property scheme would be the best investment.

While trustees are responsible for looking after your money, administrators for the day to day operations of the fund, and managers for the investment choices, this doesn't mean that it's OK for you to forget about your super. Though you can't tell trustees and investment managers what to do, there will be times when you will have to make some decisions concerning your super. It'd be nice if your super ran on auto pilot for the next 40 years so that when you retire you can pick up a cheque with a squillion noughts at the end of it. The truth is, though, that if you ignore it, you won't get nearly as much out of your super as you will if you manage it properly. In short, your decisions will have an effect on how much super you get in the end.

WHAT HAPPENS TO MY MONEY?

Your contributions, whether made by you or your employer, are invested by the managers of the fund in a variety of assets, which include property, bonds and shares. The intention is to return a profit so your money grows in value.

A concern that many have about super is the risk that is involved. All investment has an element of risk and the higher the risk, the higher the possible return. But like going to the races, if you only bet on 100/1 chances you might come up with a big win now and then but most of the time you're going to get your fingers burnt. Backing favourites, on the other hand, will give you more winners but less cash.

The idea is to balance the risk and the return so the fund will increase your account over the long term. Occasionally there will be years when a minimal return or even a loss is posted, but in other years there will be returns that are better than expected. But generally your account should grow at a reasonably steady rate. To achieve this, investment managers spread the money over a wide field of investments so that losses on one investment are balanced by gains on another.

The key to long-term saving funds, such as super, is patience. Some years you will wonder whether it's worth it when your fund does not perform well. However, in other years you will be pleasantly surprised when the fund records a better than expected performance. It might be tempting sometimes to stuff your money under the futon, but due to inflation in 40 years time that's all that today's money will be worth—stuffing. By today's standards you'd probably have to take out a personal loan to buy a meat pie and a Coke.

The bottom line is that if you want to save for your future it makes sense to invest and this is what happens to your super money.

CHAPTER 2
WHY DO I NEED SUPER?

Super is there to help you save for the future. As a rule Australians are much better at spending their bucks than saving them. One of the consequences of this habit has been that our ageing population has not put enough money away for retirement. It's a popular belief in this country, with our tradition of providing comprehensive welfare, that the government will be there for us when we are old.

With our population getting older, and therefore the proportion of Australians in the workforce decreasing, there will be increased pressure on the public purse. It's for this reason that super has been expanded by the current government to include just about everyone who picks up a shovel or taps on a keyboard. So it makes sense to look at what possibilities super can offer you.

But still it's a fair question to ask if you're single, 21 years old, earning $20000 per annum and looking at another 45 years in the workforce. Where you're going to get your money to live on in retirement is probably not the first of your priorities. You're more likely to be interested in having enough money to pay rent and support your lifestyle, and if you can buy a car or go on a holiday. You're living for now and not later.

When you're young and not earning a great deal your immediate needs are always going to be the more pressing. This doesn't mean, though, that you should reject all thoughts about your future.

IT'S NEVER TOO EARLY

But I'll finish the sermon there and get onto the facts. The earlier you start saving the better, because of the way your account earns interest. For example, imagine that your salary grew at a rate of 5 per cent per annum, your super earns a steady rate of 7 per cent interest and you contribute 5 per cent of your salary. For argument's sake let's say this person starts earning $15 000 at the age of 20, begins contributing towards super at age 25 then withdraws it at age 65. This is how your account would grow:

Age	Salary	Contributions per year	Interest per year	Accumulated amount
20	$ 15 000	—	—	—
35	$ 31 184	$1 559	$ 1 227	$ 19 542
50	$ 64 829	$3 241	$ 7 191	$ 111 539
65	$134 775	$6 739	$27 749	**$427 527**

WHY DO I NEED SUPER?

In the next example the lucky contestant begins working with the same salary at the same age. The interest is still 7 per cent a year, the salary still grows at 5 per cent a year and the contributions are a steady 5 per cent. The only difference is that contributions are first made at the age of 20 and not 25.

Age	Salary	Contributions per year	Interest per year	Accumulated amount
20	$ 5 000	$ 750	$ 26	$ 776
35	$ 31 184	$1 559	$ 1 902	$ 29 858
50	$ 64 829	$3 241	$ 9 053	$ 140 000
65	$134 775	$6 739	$32 886	**$506 052**

In this example five years worth of contributions at the start adds an extra $78 525 to the final amount. While the contributions made between the years of 20 and 25 only accumulated to $6 235, compound interest expanded the gulf between the two amounts.

One definite advantage of being young is having time on your side. If you take an interest in your super investment when you are young, it's likely to make things easier when you get older. A good place to start is to make yourself aware of what you are entitled to and how to manage your super so as to get the best return. (This will be dealt with more fully in the next chapter.)

SHOULD I PUT SOME OF MY OWN MONEY INTO SUPER?

The short answer is yes if you want to and no if you don't. It really depends on your situation, but if you are planning to rely on super for your income after retirement, then it wouldn't be a bad idea.

Perhaps the question that you should be asking yourself, if you are contemplating adding to your super, is how much money you will need in retirement. It's likely that you are going to have less expenses when you reach retirement age. Hopefully little Bruce and Raelene have grown up and moved out of home and your mortgage is paid off.

REDUCING EXPENSES BEFORE YOU RETIRE...

With this typical situation in mind, you will probably be able to support your lifestyle in retirement with an annual income around 50–75 per cent of your income prior to leaving work. It is difficult to estimate just how much you will need because it will depend on how many years you spend in retirement and what kind of lifestyle you want to lead. However, there is general agreement that the Superannuation Guarantee, even though it will rise to 9 per cent of your wage, will not be enough to provide you with this sort of income. This was one of the reasons behind the federal government's push for employee contributions, which when coupled with government contributions should add another 6 per cent, bringing compulsory super up to 15 per cent.

You may be fortunate enough to have an employer who pays more into your super than the compulsory amount. Otherwise, you might consider making your own contributions at some stage of your working life.

If you are self-employed obviously you won't be able to rely on an employer's super scheme, but it's worth your while to consider having your own super. You may be relying on the inherent value of your business which can be sold to provide money to live on in retirement. However, it is difficult to estimate what it will be worth when you retire, given the uncertainties of running a business. Those same uncertainties can lead to the collapse of your company along with a significant financial loss. It's not a thought to dwell on, but in case the unthinkable happens, super can help by providing some security for your future.

It may be that even if you have the inclination, at present you have no disposable income to put towards super. However, there is every chance that your income will grow through your working life and as this happens it may free up some money to be put away for your retirement. And there are advantages to putting money into your super fund as opposed to alternative saving schemes.

WOULDN'T I BE BETTER OFF LEAVING MY MONEY IN THE BANK?

If you want to put some of your own money away for your retirement then the bank is not the ideal place for your money. A bank account is there for the convenience of having cash at hand, not for providing good returns on a long-term investment.

The problem with leaving your money in the bank is that the interest is taxed at your marginal rate (i.e. the highest rate of income tax you pay). The interest you earn on your super fund account is taxed at the concessional rate of 15 per cent, regardless of your income. On top of this, the interest you will earn, over the long term, will be much less in a bank account than in a super fund.

Investing in super might also make you eligible for a tax rebate, currently a maximum of ten cents in the dollar (up to $100) if you earn under $31000 a year. There are also other tax incentives which will be dealt with in the next chapter.

And, finally, it simply makes good sense to add your money to an existing pool of funds because it will earn more in interest and you won't have to pay more than one set of management fees.

WHAT ABOUT INVESTING IT MYSELF?

If you choose to invest money for the future yourself, it's quite possible that you might secure a better return than if you invested in a super fund that is managed by others. However, your chances of doing so are diminished if you haven't the time to supervise your investments or the expertise, particularly as you have to overcome the disadvantage of having your returns taxed at the marginal rate you pay on your income tax, unless you set up your own personal super fund—and that involves a lot of work.

The people entrusted with managing super funds are well trained and experienced in the field of investment, as they should be because it's their job. If you're not well drilled on where the pitfalls are in investing you can get yourself into trouble. You can get around this by having someone manage your investments, but for most the cost of employing such people is too much.

Most importantly, the bigger super funds benefit from their size. With a large pool of assets at their disposal, fund managers can spread their investments over a wide area. This is called diversification and its purpose is to secure steady growth for your funds. If, for example, a poor return is recorded on property investment for the year, a good return on shares may compensate for it. Small investors, on the other hand, tend to put their money into one investment, which could be stunningly successful or on the other hand a complete disaster. The result is fluctuating fortunes and a greater degree of risk. In essence you're punting without protection.

It's natural to be suspicious of the people entrusted to look after your super, since you have never met them and it seems you have little control over what they do. While it's in your best interest to be wary, don't ignore the advantages of using super if you decide to invest money for the future. After all, if you're out at sea an ocean liner offers a smoother ride than a 12-foot dinghy.

WHY SHOULDN'T I SPEND MY MONEY NOW?

When you first start earning an income it seems cruel that some of it should be taken out and put into a retirement fund. The temptation is to spend up big. Movies, CDs, a good night out, flared pants, the choice is endless. But if you take a look at what your disposable income goes towards, you might find that a lot is spent on instant gratification—the sort of things you pay for on a whim.

'SOUND' INVESTMENTS IN THE YEAR 2040

If you are amongst the fortunate ones of this generation who have a bit of money to be frivolous with, there could be a few dollars here and there to put away for your future. Many of you may want to save but are not sure of where to get the money from. Perhaps you could come up with a bit if you gave the flares a miss. Strange as it may seem, they might be out of fashion soon.

The thing is not to approach super as a drain on your income, but as an option to consider when you think about what you do with your money. The key is to work out how best to handle it. For some, putting it into super won't be an option, but for others super makes good sense, as you'll be able to tell from the interviews contained in the second half of the book. What about you?

CHAPTER 3
HOW DO I LOOK AFTER MY SUPER?

The key to looking after your money in super is to use your common sense and to take an interest in what happens to it. From an outsider's point of view, super can seem as impenetrable as a foreign language. Rules and regulations too numerous to mention, the complex fee structures, and of course the jargon, all combine to scare the punter away. But if you avoid the brain twisting detail and keep to the basics of the industry, you'll go a long way.

To start with, have a look at the membership booklet you are provided with when you first join a fund—if you've lost yours or you didn't receive one your fund can send you another. This should tell you about the fund; whether its style is defined benefit, accumulation or a combination of the two; what type of fund—company, public offer, industry or public sector fund; the basic administration fees; and what kind of return it hopes to achieve for you. You will also receive annual reports which will detail how your fund's investments fared in the previous year and what the trustees are hoping to achieve in future years. Some funds will also publish a newsletter to keep you up to date with any new developments in the fund. It's a good idea to keep hold of the information your fund sends you, but even if you can't resist the temptation to toss it in the bin, have a read before you do it.

It's also a good idea to ask the people 'in the know' at work a few questions and go to the fund administrator. At the risk of sounding like a scratched record, always remember that the more you know, the less trouble you'll get into with your super.

HOW MUCH DO I HAVE TO PAY IN FEES?

Now we come to the ugly but necessary side of super. How much is it going to cost you?

Some of you may be lucky enough to have an employer who picks up the administration costs of your super fund. This is sometimes the case with company defined benefit funds. However, most fund members have the cost of fees deducted from their account. In such cases you could be charged for any or all of the following:

- joining the fund (known as an entry fee)
- making contributions (regular contributions tend to be

HOW DO I LOOK AFTER MY SUPER? 21

charged at a lower rate than one-off payments. Voluntary contributions are sometimes charged at a higher rate)
- maintaining your account (known as a holding or annual fee)
- an asset fee (a percentage charge of what you have in your account)
- leaving the fund (known as an exit fee)

The scale of fees will vary from fund to fund. You may find yourself having to pay other charges but these five are the main ones. How you will be charged will vary as well. Some, such as public offer funds, tend to impose most of their charges as percentages. Others, such as the industry funds, will charge a flat rate, no matter what amount of money is being dealt with. Public offer funds may also involve paying commissions to a life office agent. But again there is no set scale of fees for the super industry, so when you become a member of a fund it's a good idea to work out exactly what you have to pay.

It's difficult to say what fee level should be regarded as excessive. But certainly if the fee structure is eating into your savings then it's too much. This was a problem following the initial introduction of compulsory super, particularly in the case of small amounts. With young people tending to work in casual and part-time employment, it was common for their accounts to be swallowed by fees and taxes, especially if no contributions were coming in. To prevent this problem, the government has brought in what it calls member protection rules which operate from 1 July 1995.

Under these rules, a super fund can agree to limit its fees so as not to exceed the income from interest where the balance is less than $1000. The fund can still deduct tax and premiums for death and disability insurance. If a fund is unwilling to do this then a member's account must be transferred to a fund which offers member protection and the fund must advise the member where it has been placed. It's likely, though, that most funds will provide member protection because if they don't they are prevented under the legislation from accepting new small accounts.

However, if the employer cannot find a fund that provides member protection, and if the award or agreement allows, contributions can be paid into what is known as the Tax Office Superannuation Holding Account Reserve. The money paid into the Reserve is taxed but there are no charges above interest credited. When the balance reaches $1200 the Tax Office will inform you and suggest that you nominate a super fund to receive the money. While the Tax Office can't force you to withdraw the money it's a good idea to get it out at this point because these holding accounts do not work like super funds and do not offer death and disability cover like most super funds. The Tax Office hangs on to your money until you are ready for it

HOW DO I LOOK AFTER MY SUPER?   23

to be transferred into the super system. You can't make your own contributions and the interest your money will earn while it's being held by the Tax Office will be minimal and no interest is paid on the amount in excess of $1200.

Your boss should let you know if your super is being paid in this way, but failing this, or if your super from a previous job has been put into one of these accounts, the Tax Office will let you know when money has been given to it on your behalf. Keep an eye on your money if it's in a Tax Office account because when $1200 is reached it's better off in the super system, but it will only be transferred when you request it.

HOW DO I FIND OUT WHAT FEES I HAVE TO PAY?

Super funds must disclose their fees and charges to their fund members, but of course some will be better than others at keeping you up to date. For example, some funds only provide their members with annual reports and statements while others put out regular newsletters as well. This material should tell you about administration fees but if you are still unsure, talk to your employer or the fund administrator.

WHAT ABOUT TAXES?

When it comes to taxes, the situation is clearer, but we're not talking crystal clear, not by any stretch of the imagination. The waters are certainly a lot murkier if you received super before July 1983 when the tax arrangement was very different. However, most of you won't be in this boat, and so, essentially, tax comes into play at three points in the super system:

Contributions

Those made by your employer are taxed at 15 per cent, while the contributions you make yourself are tax free. This is because these contributions are made from money from which income tax has already been paid. But while your employer is entitled to a tax deduction on super contributions up to a certain limit, you are not. However, as discussed in the previous chapter, you are entitled to a small rebate for your contributions if your income is under $31 000 p.a.

If you are self-employed, you will receive a full tax deduction on the first $3000 you contribute to your super each year, then a 75 per cent deduction up to the limit that is set for your age, which will be detailed later in the chapter.

Investment earnings

Investment earnings are taxed at 15 per cent right across the board, but are offset to some extent by deductions for costs incurred in the administration of the fund and prior taxation of dividends before they are passed on to you as earnings.

Benefits

Current arrangements are that when you receive your benefit, the first $83 168 is absolutely tax free. No questions asked, satisfaction guaranteed, and a set of those groovy steak knives chucked in at no extra cost. This amount will increase in line with average weekly earnings. On top of this, the amount of contributions you made from after-tax income during your working life is tax free as well. Apart from this the amount in excess of $83 168 is taxed at 15 per cent (plus Medicare levy) which for a lump sum is payable when you get it. If you receive a pension, tax is taken out of each payment. This applies until the amount reaches what is called the Reasonable Benefit Limit. The limit will vary, depending on what form you take your benefit in, but the amount of your benefit over this limit is taxed at the top marginal rate which is currently 47 per cent (plus the Medicare levy). The Reasonable Benefit Limit is explained in more detail in the next chapter.

WHAT DO I DO IF I LEAVE MY JOB?

Chances are that you will change your job at some stage during your life and that you will do it more than once. You might have just finished some part-time work that kept you breathing while studying or learning a trade, or perhaps you've switched jobs in your chosen career. Leaving a job, however, doesn't mean you forfeit your super benefit along with your locker key.

When you leave a job, the money your employer has contributed to your fund, along with any payments you might have made yourself, plus investment earnings, less taxes and fees, needs to be fixed up. In most cases the fund will contact you and ask you what you want to do with your money, otherwise you will have to get in contact with the fund administrators yourself. You may choose to do nothing with it in which case your money will be left where it is.

Generally your money must stay in super until you reach retirement, so when you leave employment you can't take it out because it is 'preserved'. There are some exceptions to this in that certain circumstances will allow you to withdraw your super benefit before you reach 65 (these will be dealt with in Chapter 4). Also when you leave employment you can sometimes get your money if the total amount is less than $500 when you leave a fund or if you have contributed your own money in voluntary contributions, in which case some funds will allow you to withdraw these amounts from your super.

Chances are that you will want your money rolled over. This dubious sounding manoeuvre simply means that you wish it to be transferred to another fund. If you want to roll over all your money, your new fund should be able to give you a form authorising them to do the work for you. This streamlined service is very new and it only applies if you are moving all your money, so in some cases you may be sent a statement of termination payment form or STP (it sounds ominous but it just means you've left the fund) and a roll-over payment notification form or RPN. You sign these forms and nominate a receiving fund and the money will be paid into your new fund.

If some time after you've left your old job you join a new fund there is still the opportunity to roll over your old super into your present fund.

There are circumstances when it is less convenient, or not possible, to roll over your super.

If you belong to an industry fund, and you're changing your job to another within the same industry, then your new employer might use the same fund. In this case, the contributions you receive from your new job can be added to the account you had with your old job. This will save you the hassle of shifting money about.

With some defined benefit style funds, you may be unable to take your super with you as they keep hold of your benefit until you retire. On the other side of the coin, if you start a job with an employer who uses a defined benefit style super fund, it may not be designed to accept super rolled over from an accumulation style fund.

In other cases you might find that if your employer is paying super above the award or Super Guarantee, you won't receive the difference from your fund when you resign because you haven't worked for long enough. This occurs mostly in the case of employer-sponsored funds and it is the employer's right. Employers hold this part of their employees' super back as an incentive to keep them loyal to the company. Often workers have to wait 5 or 10 years before their employer's contributions, paid on top of the compulsory amount, are fully 'vested' (the industry term which means you are entitled to all the super contributed on your behalf).

However, most of you will have to roll over your super at some point during your working life. This area of super arguably causes the punter the most problems, but they can be avoided and the rules are getting simpler.

CAN I STILL ADD TO MY SUPER IF I LEAVE THE WORKFORCE?

Many people will experience time away from work when they are young. It may be due to unemployment, a career change, study, travel, or maternity. Whatever the reason, it is not unusual for you to find that after working for a few years you have some time off. But even though you might be out of paid employment it's important that you don't forget your super.

One of the most common reasons for women to leave paid work is to have and look after children. With the increased participation of women in the workforce it is clear that for many families the days of the husband being the sole financial provider are over and things are likely to be the same when we get to retirement age.

In recognition of this and the fact that more men are taking time off work to look after their children, under super regulations and provided the fund trust deed allows it, people can take unpaid parental leave and maintain their super fund via voluntary contributions for up to 7 years. Most of you will probably not spend this much time out of work if you wish to return to your former job, but the facility is there to ensure that women who have children, and their families, are not inconvenienced because of it.

If you leave work for other reasons—study, unemployment etc—voluntary contributions can be made for two years. Even if you leave the workforce for an extended period and you don't intend to return to your old job, it may not necessarily be the case that you must transfer your super to a new fund. If you belong to an industry fund and will be working in the same field when you go back to work then you might be able to leave your money sitting in your account so you can pick up where you left off on your return. Ask your fund administrator to see if this is possible.

If you know that you will not be able to use your current account when you next have a job then you should take steps to preserve the super you have until you are next earning an income. There are many options open for you on transferring your super to a personal fund but it's a question of picking the right one. To help you make a decision, you should get some financial advice you can trust. (See the section For more information on p. 75.)

WHAT DO I DO IF I'VE LOST MY SUPER?

Put up wanted posters. If they don't work, you're stuffed.

In all seriousness though, the truth is that your super never gets lost, rather it's you that does the disappearing act. But there are ways to find you and your funds again.

The government requires that funds make an effort to find a member after two annual reports or newsletters have not been received (usually this is discovered when they are returned through the mail). If the fund is unsuccessful in tracking you down then your benefit must be protected from fees and charges or it may be placed in an eligible roll-over fund to protect it from fees and taxes. From 1 July 1996, the fund supplies your details to the Tax Office which keeps a record of the location of unclaimed benefits.

If you want to find your super from a previous job then you can start by asking:

- your present fund, as they might have records of your transactions with other funds
- your employer from that time
- the Tax Office as it will have details of any benefits held for you by a fund and there is a chance your super is or has been paid into their Superannuation Holding Account Reserve scheme.

However, it's not hard to get around the problem of locating your benefits if you take two simple steps. First, make sure when you join a fund that you keep a record of which institution acts as the fund manager as well as your membership number. And secondly, you should let them know when you change your address. That way it's you and your benefits until death do you part, and all that.

DO I HAVE A SAY IN HOW MY SUPER IS INVESTED?

Basically it depends on which fund you belong to. There is a push to open up funds to 'member investment choice' as it is termed and some already offer their members the option of choosing from a range of different investment strategies, while others invest on the basis of what they think are the members' best interests. The law will not allow member investment choice to the extent that you can pick and choose exactly which shares are bought and what real estate venture is invested in. That would add new meaning to the word chaos.

HOW DO I LOOK AFTER MY SUPER?

> OK LOVE! WHICH INVESTMENT STRATEGY WOULD YOU LIKE?

> AS LONG AS HE HAS TIGHT SHORTS I DON'T CARE...

Generally, the way funds offer member investment choice is by presenting a range of investment strategies which differ in the level of risk involved. For example, there might be three or four separate portfolios which offer a different balance between risk and return. Some funds will allow you to divide your money amongst the various 'baskets' while others ask you to choose one above the others.

If you are offered member investment choice and you don't inform the fund manager which investment style you desire then usually an investment strategy is chosen on your behalf, and for young people most funds would invest the money according to a high growth, higher risk strategy. However, it's worth your while to think about what kind of investment you would prefer, when given the choice, if for no other reason than increasing your knowledge of, and control over, what happens to your money.

CAN I CHOOSE WHICH SUPER FUND MY MONEY GOES INTO?

If you are not covered by an award which designates a particular fund as the recipient, then it depends on your employer. Nearly all will have a particular fund they pay their employees' contributions into, but some employers will agree to use a fund that you have from a previous job or a personal super fund that you started yourself. However, this is a rare thing as most employers regard it as an inconvenience, particularly if it is a large company with many employees.

A situation which is not uncommon, particularly for people who change jobs regularly, is to have a personal fund, whether it be for storing rolled-over super or to serve as an active super fund in conjunction with their current employer's fund. On resigning from a job, the super is rolled over into the personal fund. For many this represents a convenient way to organise their super while moving from job to job. The downside is the likelihood that having two super accounts open at once will cost you more in administration fees.

HOW DO RELATIONSHIPS AFFECT MY SUPER?

With regard to relationships, super becomes an issue in the situation of death and divorce.

In the case of death a payment which is the balance of your super account can be made to one or more of the following:

- your husband or wife (including a de facto)
- your children

- anyone who is financially dependent on you
- your estate (which means it will be distributed according to your will).

The rules of the fund will usually state who gets paid.

If your fund pays to your estate, it is important if you are in a gay or lesbian relationship and you want the benefit paid to your partner in the case of your death, that you ensure you have an up to date will indicating that this is your wish.

In the case of divorce, super is a bit of an odd one out for the family court. The family court has pretty wide powers to distribute marital property; however, with super it is difficult because while it is an asset it can't be got at until retirement. This makes it a tricky one to divide up. There are a variety of ways the court has dealt with this, including direct payments and giving the non-super-owning party a larger share of assets.

The problem is that the Family Court really hasn't caught up with super—in fact the federal government is considering amending the Family Law Act to deal with it—so it is a good idea if you are going through divorce and you or your partner have a significant amount of money in super to get some legal and financial advice.

WHAT DO I DO IF I'M SELF-EMPLOYED?

If you are self-employed and interested in having super for yourself, then a personal account in a super fund may be the solution. Most do this by contributing to a public offer fund. Alternatively you can start a super fund of your own with its own trust deed. This will give you maximum control over what happens to your money but you will not benefit from the economies of scale that come from investing with a large pool of money.

If you wish to start a personal super fund, whatever the type, make sure you find out about all the costs involved. It's a bit like getting your car repaired at the mechanics. If you show them you know a thing or two by asking the right questions then they're likely to tell you more about what's going on. It must be said, however, that most agents will comply with disclosure regulations and tell you what you need to know.

In these cases it's a good idea for the self-employed to get some credible, and independent, financial advice. (See the section For more information on p. 75.)

Being self-employed entitles you to a full tax deduction for the first $3000 you contribute to your super fund each year, and thereafter 75 per cent up to a limit which is set according to how old you are:

Age at end of the year	Maximum deductible contributions per year (indexed to average weekly earnings)
Under 35	$ 9 405
35–49	$26 125
50 and over	$64 790

Many who run their own show are conscious of building its value and so re-invest much of their income back into the business rather than put it away for retirement. If this is so it may be a way to save for your future but you must consider how much your business is worth and whether selling it will provide you with a livable income in retirement. If not, then super is there as an option for you to consider.

As mentioned in the previous chapter, there is also the prospect to consider of your business going under. Not a pleasant thought but there is always the possibility of it happening. If you invest all you have back into the shop you're left with nothing if the business fails. Super can offer a way to spread your assets out and make things a little more secure for your future, particularly as there are laws against using super to invest in your own company.

IS MY MONEY SAFE IN SUPER?

Safety is a relative concept because you can never discount chance. So if you were to ask me if it is more likely that the sun will rise tomorrow than you getting your super I'd have to say yes. But if you asked whether it was more likely that a rock fall out of the sky and pancake your car then I'd say no.

It might look like beating around the bush but chance and risk are never far away when you're talking about money and investment. It is part and parcel of making your money grow and, if managed well, risk will ultimately be to your benefit in the shape of healthy returns on your investments. And through diversification of investment your super fund cuts the chances of sustaining a loss to a minimum. The idea is that over time the returns will outweigh the losses.

To help minimise the risk, there are strict rules specified in recent government legislation on what a super fund can and cannot do with your money. They include:

- a fund cannot act like a bank and lend money to people
- borrowing by funds is not allowed, except for unexpected short-term cash needs and then only on the condition that the money is repaid within a specified time
- a fund must keep its investments separate from the assets of the company if it is a company fund. The reason for this is that it keeps your super out of harm's way if your employer goes bust
- a fund is required by law to develop an investment strategy, approved by the trustees, which the investment managers must adhere to.

The effect of these regulations, along with the supervision of trustees, the involvement of the Insurance and Superannuation Commission as the industry regulator, and the competence of those charged with managing your fund's investments, is to ensure that it is extremely unlikely that you will lose your money in the long run.

This being so, it's still not fun to think that you're taking a risk with your livelihood, but it is important to look at super in broader terms. Our collective prosperity depends in large part on the performance of the economy. To this end, super not only delivers the goods when we retire but also during our working lives. Close to $200 billion at the time of publication of this book is invested in super funds and the pool of money is on the increase all the time. Most of this money is invested in Australia which is a major support for the economy. Judiciously invested super has the potential to help our economy grow and in turn provide for our wellbeing in the best possible way—by creating jobs.

WHAT DO I DO IF I HAVE A PROBLEM WITH MY SUPER?

If you're uncertain, the last thing to do is to shrug your shoulders and forget about it. Procedures are in place and people appointed to deal with your queries and concerns. Use them, because the more you know about your super, the better. But to use them effectively it's important to work out who is responsible for your problem: your employer or the fund itself.

If your concern is with the administration of your account then the first thing to do is to get in contact with the fund administrators and make some inquiries. The cost of fees and taxes, the balance of your account, early pay outs for death, disability etc are the sorts of things the administrator is responsible for.

If you are still unhappy after talking with the fund administrators, and you feel you have a genuine complaint, you don't have to shove pins into voodoo dolls—there are far more effective means at your disposal.

IT'S NEVER TOO EARLY

The trustees' role, as mentioned earlier, is to look after your interests as the member. They are the people in the fund who ultimately deal with your complaint. Every fund with 5 members or more must, by law, set up its own complaints procedures to resolve disputes. Normally your fund has 90 days to deal with your complaint. If the trustees don't resolve the matter to your satisfaction, then the option may be open for you to pass the matter on to the Superannuation Complaints Tribunal, a body established as the watchdog for the super industry. Generally you must take your complaint to the tribunal within 12 months of the fund's decision.

The Tribunal may well agree with the decision of the trustees; however, if it feels you have a genuine complaint it may ask you and the trustees to meet so as to achieve some conciliation. The Tribunal can also ask the trustees to vary their decision. If the fund sticks its head in the sand and won't do as the Tribunal asks, the Insurance and Superannuation Commission (ISC) may step in. The ISC is a government body charged with regulating the insurance and super industries and is equipped with certain powers to intervene in the operation of a fund. These include the ability to obtain a court action to force the fund to abide by the Tribunal's decision and, if it is a serious breach, the ISC can also launch an investigation of the fund.

However, if you have a problem with your employer, for example you are not being paid the correct amount of super, then the situation is slightly different. Instead of being a concern for the super industry it is an industrial matter. The employer also has obligations under tax law. How you go about dealing with it depends on the circumstances.

If you feel that your employer is making an honest mistake then your best bet is probably to go directly to your boss. However, in many cases this won't be possible, particularly if you feel your employer is pulling a shifty by not paying your super. Union members have the recourse to go to their representative and ask them to negotiate on their behalf, but those not unionised won't have this option. If you're not in a union then it's a good idea to get in contact with bodies such as the Tax Office to get help with your particular problem.

There is the chance that the Tax Office will pick up the discrepancy through running an audit on the company, or you yourself can inform them that you're not getting your super by filling out a form that is available from any Tax Office. If the Tax Office discovers that your company hasn't paid enough super, or none at all, it charges the company the balance on behalf of you and your workmates. When the money is retrieved from the company, it is placed in holding accounts under your names and the Tax Office will then tell you that the money is waiting for you. (See the section For more information on p. 75.)

CHAPTER 4
WHEN DO I GET MY MONEY?

Generally, you are paid your benefit when you retire, and currently the super industry observes 65 as the retirement age. So if you're twenty in 1995 you'll be cashing in your chips in the year 2040.

You may well be thinking that it's just a tad irrelevant to be discussing a super pay out that you will receive in four or five decades time, but super doesn't begin when you get old, it begins with your first job. While it might feel like the money in your super plan is nothing more than figures on a piece of paper, it's important to remember that it will be returned to you at some point in the future. Thinking about what you're going to get when you retire is natural enough, but you also have to think about what you want to get. Do this and before you know it you'll be one of those sensible types who always remembers garbage night, squeezes the toothpaste from the bottom of the tube, and has a healthy super account. Or maybe you can settle for one out of three.

However, while most of you will get your super when you say goodbye to the punch clock, there are certain circumstances which allow an exception to the rule that you must wait until 65 to get your money. Even if you don't think retirement should enter into your thinking at this stage of the game, the situations which permit an early pay out definitely should. They are:

Early retirement

Although 65 is the generally observed retirement age, it is possible for you to receive your benefits earlier than this. You can retire and receive your benefits up to 10 years before you turn 65 if you prove that you are leaving the workforce permanently.

Some defined benefit funds will reduce your benefit by a certain percentage for each year under the retirement age used in the fund rules. With accumulation plans there is no penalty but you have sacrificed several years worth of contributions to spend a longer time in retirement. If you do retire early you will have to be confident that your super, combined with any social security you are entitled to, will be enough to keep you going.

Disablement

One of the benefits of super is that your plan may also provide you with insurance cover. This means that if you are unable to work because of illness or injury then your super fund can give you a disablement benefit. Some plans will provide this automatically while others will charge you a small levy according to how much cover you wish to have.

If it is agreed that you will never be able to work again—in some cases this will be obvious while in others more extensive medical assessment will be required by the fund—most defined benefit plans will pay you an amount equal to what you would have received had you worked until normal retirement age. With accumulation plans, nearly all of them will pay you what is already in your fund, but some will also pay a set amount which is usually determined by your age. Generally, it will decrease the closer you get to retirement. The reasoning behind this is that the older you are, the more money you are likely to have saved in your super account.

If you are deemed to be temporarily disabled then some funds (in particular company funds) may also make payments from super to help keep you going until you're back on your feet. In such cases trustees must decide whether you are entitled to payments, if so how much, and at what point they should stop. This would involve medical assessment of your condition. If the trustees agree that you qualify for temporary disability payments, your benefit is likely to be paid as a pension while you are out of the work-force, off-set by any workers' compensation you might be receiving as well.

When there are claims of permanent and temporary disability there will sometimes be disagreement. Insurance companies and superannuation funds don't want to be taken for a ride by fraudulent claims, but people forced out of work need their money. These interests occasionally come into conflict. Most disputes are settled by the fund and the member but some will be resolved by the Superannuation Complaints Tribunal as mentioned in the previous chapter.

In applying for disability payments from your super fund and in the process of dealing with your claim, the trustees are bound by confidentiality. That is, it's illegal for them to discuss your case with anyone else.

A drawback with the disability cover super funds offer is the wait after you become unable to work before the payment of benefits, which can sometimes take up to 6 months. This aside, superannuation can be one way of putting up a safety net for yourself without the hassle and cost of taking out an insurance policy.

Death

As well as providing for disablement, some super funds will also pay a special benefit to the dependants of a member if he or she dies, as well as paying the balance of the account. Usually, it's an amount equal to that paid in the case of permanent disability, but it will vary from fund to fund. Who receives the payment will usually be decided by the trustees, who will look at who is stated to be the recipient in the beneficiary nomination form that some funds will ask you to sign when you join. But as discussed in the previous chapter (How do relationships affect my super, p. 32) it may ultimately depend upon your will if the benefit is paid to the estate.

Financial hardship

The trust deeds of most funds will allow the release of benefits to their members if they are suffering from severe financial hardship and the ISC determines that they are in need. To get hold of your money you must have ceased making or receiving contributions and provided the Insurance and Superannuation Commission with documentation that you have no other means to pay your debts. If the Commissioner is satisfied that you are in desperate need of your money to cover debts and expenses, you'll be allowed to have access to your super benefit if the trust deed allows such payments.

Emigration

Your plan will usually release your benefits if you are emigrating permanently. However, you must give sufficient proof that you are moving overseas for good, such as deeds of sale of your local assets, employment contracts in the country you are going to and so on.

Getting hold of your super before you reach the normal retirement age might seem overly complicated but there is a reason for all these restrictions. The purpose of superannuation is not to be a pool of money which you dip into at your leisure; rather, its role is to provide you with an income during retirement. In the next 40 or so years there might be a time when you will need to draw on your funds, but the government has decided that in the main your money should be preserved in super until you leave work for good.

HOW IS IT PAID TO ME?

When the time comes for you to receive your super benefit, you could well be paid in two ways. You either receive a lump sum (i.e. a thumping great cheque) or a pension. Alternatively, you may get a combination between the two, part of it lump sum and part of it pension. It might seem like much of a muchness but there are differences between the two.

Pensions

The situation with pensions is fairly straightforward. Currently, when you retire your fund will pay your benefit as a set amount at regular intervals for the rest of your life. The risk and responsibility of managing your money is taken on by your super fund.

Lump sums

With lump sums all your money, quite literally, is in your hands. The responsibility for its management, as well as the risk, is borne by you. You may want to spend it all immediately on a holiday home or a trip overseas or, as most people choose to do, invest it again to secure a steady income.

Currently, people who want to invest their lump sums in order to get a regular income often choose to invest in an annuity or an allocated pension from one financial institution or another. Annuities and allocated pensions are similar in many ways but do have one important difference. An allocated pension will last only as long as the money does, whereas an annuity can be paid for the rest of your life.

Taking a lump sum will give you many more options as to what to do with your benefit. However, it can also have the result that you pay more tax through what is called the Reasonable Benefit Limit (RBL).

The RBL has been set by government legislation at $418 000, which will rise in the future in accordance with average weekly earnings. Your benefit will be taxed at the concessional rate up to this amount (disregarding the first $83 168 of your benefit and your own contributions which are tax free) but any money you receive from your benefit which exceeds the RBL will be taxed at the top marginal rate. However, if you receive at least half of your benefit in the form of a pension then the RBL is set, in today's dollars, at $836 000.

This may present some problems but most of you won't exceed the RBL. The question that you will be presented with is more likely to be what to do with a lump-sum payment—whether you should buy an annuity or invest it in some other way. Since you're pondering your financial security it would make sense to get some credible financial advice. Better that than blowing it all by going into partnership with a mate who's a worm farmer.

Another thing to remember is that future governments, in all their wisdom, may change the rules of the game again. When it is time for you to retire, the situation is likely to be different from today's. The key is to be aware of how any changes to the payment of super benefits will affect your plans for retirement.

WILL I GET THE PENSION?

The answer to that question is probably no, at least not the full amount. The current government's policy is to provide social security in retirement only when a person does not have enough savings of their own. And to this end super is being encouraged. Of course, so much is bound to happen between now and then it's just about impossible to make predictions about what will happen to the aged pension. Currently the pension is paid subject to an income and assets test and, just as an indication of what applies, the pension is reduced by half the amount of income earned over the threshold. As at 1 July 1995 the income thresholds are set at $45 per week for singles and $39 per week for partners (each).

It's fair to say that none of the major political parties appear to be thinking about introducing a universal pension for the over 60s because the cost would be too great for the nation. More likely is a move in the other direction towards more restricted access.

By world standards, Australia's aged pension is quite generous, but it's no secret that one of the main reasons the federal government has given super the big push in the last few years is the realisation that in a generation the country will be struggling to support the aged in the way it does today, through benefits paid from current tax collections.

It's only natural to suspect that as more people reach the pension age, resources will be spread more thinly. This might seem an alarming prediction, but it's balanced by the likelihood that as a result of the introduction of compulsory super most of us will have more money saved for retirement than our parents had. Social security might be more restricted than it is today but fewer people will be needing it. The World Bank has recently given Australia a big tick for the way we are planning for an ageing population. Compulsory super savings plus voluntary super savings, backed up by a social security pension is the way to go.

INTERVIEWS

Dani-lea

Dani-lea is 21 years old and fortunate enough to work for a company which offers its employees a generous super fund.

> I always know roughly how much each company has contributed. Other companies I've worked for have contributed just the compulsory amount but at the moment my super is 17 per cent of my pay and if you add more they give you more towards it.

Dani-lea works for a major investment group, so it is not surprising that its employees are offered a good super fund. Previously she worked in hospitality where she was usually paid the minimum amount. Currently her job is organising functions and meetings but she has recently earned a promotion to the position of purchasing coordinator.

Dani-lea is happy with her job and hopes to continue working for her employer for some time. The generous super fund is certainly one of the reasons she doesn't have itchy feet, particularly as she feels that super is likely to be her only source of income in retirement.

> I think it's a good thing as probably by the time we get older we're going to need our super because there won't be a pension.

But also, at times, she understandably feels that it would be nice to have the money at her fingertips.

> I know it's important that we save now but sometimes it'd be nice to take it out if you're below the quota of $500 when you leave the job.
> You don't think that bit of money will make a difference when you're older.

Dani-lea has also learnt through her own experience the difficulties involved in looking after your super.

> I'm still trying to chase up super from my old job that I left a year ago, because I wasn't aware of what happened to my super or how to roll it over. I thought that when you start a new job it would be automatically rolled over into my new fund.
> I only found out later through my new job that I had to do something about it when they asked me if I wanted to roll my super over.

Dani-lea feels that more needs to be done by way of education.

> I think it would be good for young people, or anybody for that matter, to be made aware of what to do with that super, to roll it over or whatever, when they leave a job.
> Super funds should do more to let you know what options you have.

Dani-lea concedes that if she wasn't working for a company with such a generous policy on super she wouldn't be putting as much into her super, however she is still enthusiastic about super.

> We're all going to need it some day and I think I'll have to rely on it as my only support.

Tony

Tony is 25 years old, has an economics degree, and has just completed the final exams for the Solicitor Admissions Board law course. Being a student for some seven years meant that Tony had to do his fair share of part-time work. His first job was pulling beers in a pub but he first came across super in his second job.

> I took a part-time job with a book shop which paid me the compulsory super into REST, which is the retail industry fund.
>
> I didn't contribute any of my own money because working part time you want as much money in your pocket, the return for putting it into super seems very distant.

Tony's view of super is that it's a good idea in principle that has some drawbacks in practice.

> It gives people the discipline to save but you wonder how effective it is when you read in the paper how badly super funds performed in the last 12 months.
>
> There is a role for super but I don't think it should be compulsory and I don't know that it is for everyone.
>
> There needs to be choice. I think making broad sweeping legislation and setting rates—which when they increase will be very high—after employers have paid workers' compensation premiums, pay-roll tax and of course the wage, super is another cost. Perhaps it should be bargained on a person-by-person basis instead of being across the board.

Tony believes that people wanting to find out more about super are handicapped by a lack of information.

> I think most people know that there are tax benefits to be gained from super but it's not as simple as it's made out to be.

> In the two years I was working I got one letter saying how much money was in my super account and I had absolutely no knowledge of what was going on.
> Of course a lot of it was eaten up by fees because the amounts being contributed were quite small.

While Tony is suspicious of how super funds operate he still regards saving, and particularly investment, as a good thing. Though he comes from the bush, he intends to work as a practising lawyer in the city and provide for his retirement by managing his own investments.

> I don't think I will be relying on my super, I see it as some sort of a bonus.
> I see myself as having the discipline to save money and invest it in things that I think are worthwhile by following the (stock) market. I'd like to do it that way rather than leaving it to someone else—that's what I have trouble with.

Despite not being a fan of super, Tony intends to take an interest in what happens to the money in his super account and any changes and developments in the coming years so as to get the most out of it than he can.

> I think it's a good idea to consolidate your money as you move from job to job because it will earn more in interest. Also I think it would be good to give people greater say in how they'd like it done.
> Where super is a good thing is that it gives people something for retirement but you still have to give everyone an element of choice. Some may choose to have someone else run their investments totally but it would be good to allow people to control what happens to their money to some degree.

Tony agrees that retirement is something that's far from your mind when you're young but that it should be something to give some thought to. He feels that many are turned off super because they can't get at their money.

> I think young people would love to be able to withdraw their funds when retirement seems so distant. I think it's a good idea, though, to start thinking about retirement at an early age. I'm not sure that starting it with compulsory contributions as soon as people get their first job is such a good idea, it just depends on how much time people will need to build up enough money for their retirement.

Nerissa

Nerissa has a good old chuckle when asked if she would classify herself as a saver or a spender.

> I am a spender, a full-on spender. How much have I saved in the whole time I've worked? Three hundred dollars—and I did that last week.

Nerissa is 24 and has recently taken up a full-time position as a media relations officer for the same company that has employed her to operate their computer data base since 1992. Previously she worked as a waitress when she was at university.

You could safely say that retirement is not a word that Nerissa regularly drops into conversation.

> When people say the word retirement I think it's irrelevant, it's too far away to think about. I think of picket fences, the country, really bad stuff.

For the time being, Nerissa plans to start a graduate diploma course in public relations next year and she is currently studying Maltese, her mother's language.

Despite not giving retirement much thought she is very much interested in her super. She doesn't think of it so much as her retirement income, but more as an amount of money that is hers to look after.

> There was some sort of law that came in requiring the employer to pay super and that was the year that I started work for my current boss so it's always been there. I got a statement in December telling me I had a $1000 in my super. I'd probably last two weeks on that.
>
> I think, though, that super is a must for me personally.

While Nerissa is not rushing around and arranging her finances for the future, she is conscious that the time will come when she will have to consider what she does with her money a little more carefully.

> Up until I'm 26 I want to have a really good time. Thirty is the age that I think I'll have to get serious but until then I'm not even contemplating the future.

She is also conscious that planning for her future is her responsibility.

> But it will be up to me to plan for my future. I don't

rely on anyone for anything. So when it comes to super I would never even contemplate anyone supporting me, be it a husband, be it a partner, be it anyone else. I'm going to be supporting myself through working, so therefore it's logical that I will be supporting myself in my old age.

While Nerissa looks towards super as the form of saving she will be using for her retirement, like most of us she has her doubts about it.

I'm not sure about the push towards super though. Most people in society are working OK? So in, say, 40 years time when we are retiring, most people will have super but there will be a proportion of the community who don't.
From our standpoint now that's normal, but when you are going to have a culture that is totally super-oriented, where is that small proportion of people going to fit in? Will the pension still be around?

Nerissa thinks there will still be welfare for the aged but that access to it will be restricted and recipients will have to deal with a stigma associated with the pension similar to that which other people on welfare have to deal with.

The reality is that it's something that has to be done because the government can't afford to keep providing everyone with pensions. But what will the effect be?

Nerissa is also worried about how safe her money is.

I know that money gets invested and I'm a bit suss of it. My parents lost some money in an investment so I'm not sure how secure a super investment is.
I think we should be told more about what's happening to our money. All I got was a letter telling me what I had in my account, it didn't say anything about what they did with the money.

These doubts aside, Nerissa's opinion is that super is a necessity.

> I think it's great that the employer is paying compulsory super. Super is important because where else are people going to get their money from?

Chris

Chris has just started working part time as a pub cellar man and at 21 has already worked in the hospitality industry for 3 years and wants to make a career out of it. Even though he is not in a full-time job with his current employer, Chris hopes that he will soon be offered the position of bottle-shop manager.

> I applied to do a diploma in tourism and hospitality, but I talked to a lot of people doing the course and they said that everything I'm doing here is what they were going to teach me, so they wouldn't be able to tell me anything new.

While Chris feels he is learning enough about managing pubs on the job, he likes the idea of doing a course that will help him invest in pubs and hotels.

> I'm going to try and do an investment course because I'm interested in getting shares in pubs, but at the moment I don't have much idea about how to do it, it's just a thing in my mind. I've played around with some mining shares which were about 4 or 500 [dollars] worth.
> That's the only way to make some real money, I think, by investing in something.

Chris was paid super at his previous jobs but hasn't kept track of all his money because it's in separate accounts.

> I was in Host Plus [the hospitality industry plan] for two pubs and with another went through ANZ.
> I just filled in the forms and said 'yeah, whatever'. I've got something like $36.50 in that one so I haven't taken much notice of it.

Even though he hasn't taken a lot of interest in super up until now, Chris reckons that it will play a part in his future.

> I think I should start thinking about it. I've decided that working in pubs is the way to go, this is what I plan to do for the next 10 or 15 years.
> I think with compound interest it makes sense to start thinking about investing in super now. But when can you touch it though? That's the only thing in the long run that might be a problem.

Chris says that he doesn't think much at all about retirement and argues that most other people in his age group would feel the same way. However, he can see the virtues of starting to make some plans.

> It's a pretty important thing, when you think about it. My old man is about 7 or 8 years off retiring and he's only really started to think about it now. He's going through the stress of it and he talks about what he did do, or what he didn't do when he was my age.

As he mentioned, Chris will look to invest to make some money for himself but will also rely on his super for some security. However, he'd like to have more involvement in the decisions made about where his super is invested. He also thinks that the idea of compulsory employee super has both good and bad points.

> With the pressure that there will be on our social security system with everyone getting older, it's definitely a good idea [that people are made to save]

but then again you should still have some choice I suppose. It's a hard one.

Chris is aware of the difference between public offer funds and industry funds, having been in both, and thinks the latter are much more convenient.

> It's definitely better having a hospitality fund and then there is super for the building industry and the others. It's better this way because otherwise I'd have to go through the hassle of moving my super and sometimes it's not easy.

Chris would like to know more about the details of super but would prefer it if it was a little easier to understand. But at the end of the day he views super as a necessity. As he said himself, investing is the way to make real money.

Superna

Superna is a radio journalist who has worked for the ABC and currently produces a national public radio show focused on third world issues. At 28 she has been receiving super for 3 years.

> We were informally asked to be part of this fund—it's not paid into the media industry fund but a private one instead.

One concern that Superna has is what is motivating the government to implement compulsory super. She has her doubts that it is a better idea than the pension.

> . . . in terms of people knowing what super is about. With pensions it's kind of open, you know what to expect. The government is providing for you and it's pretty clear, but

> in super there are so many grey areas that when you do retire you can find yourself in a bit of a trap because you didn't read the fine print.
> That happened to my father; when he retired he had to pay another $7000 of his savings into this package. It's pretty scary because he's very thorough, he's really conscious of his own financial matters.
> But basically with super it seems that it's left to people themselves to deal with it and I don't think that should be the way, the government has some responsibility as well.

Superna admits that she doesn't take much interest in her super because she sees retirement too far down the track to be of concern and also because her father has usually given her financial advice. However, she is aware that some day this will change.

> My father has always been good with stuff like that but I know he's not going to be around forever and that it's something I have to think about sooner rather than later. For the last few years I've started to do my own tax returns and so I've become more aware of money matters but I have a tendency to think that someone will be there if I get into trouble.

Superna is not sure that compulsory employee contributions are a great idea—she would prefer it if people had the option to choose—but likes the fact that some funds offer their members insurance cover.

> I think it's good that some of them have that flexibility. It's something there should be more of.

Vince

Vince is 19 and has recently begun a job as a distribution trainee with a company that delivers food stuffs to restaurants around the country. For the next three years Vince will be learning the ins and outs of distribution both on the job and at TAFE, where he takes a course two nights a week.

This is Vince's first job and so obviously the first time he has been paid super.

> It's good for the government, because, from what I have done in economics at school, they won't have to pay the pension later on. And I suppose for us, knowing that you are going to have a certain amount of money when you retire is good too.
>
> I haven't thought about how it will affect me though because it's too far off.

While Vince hasn't started to think about what super he will have when he retires, he says this has got more to do with not being told about it than not having an inclination to find out.

> You know that you're being paid it because it's on your pay slip but that's about it really.

Vince admits that there is not much more he knows about his super than that. He isn't sure what rate he is paid, how much he has and what fund it is being paid into.

While he doesn't claim to be an expert, he makes the point that it will be hard to sell low-income earners the idea that they should contribute their own money to super as it's a bit rich to ask them to save when they need as much money in their pockets as they can get.

> They're still getting taxed and they still know that people now are getting the pension and I suppose they

figure 'Why should I contribute if people like me are still getting the pension?'

However, Vince says he will consider contributing his own money.

> I'll put some in because, I suppose, it's knowing that your own future is going to be all right, you know that you are protecting it—like saving for a house or something like that.

He also reckons that if employees will contribute to their company super fund with their own money, it will have to be done before they get their pay.

> When you're young, the short term outweighs the long term, but if your employer takes it out for you it might work, because if you get the cash in your hand, chances are you're going to spend it on something else before you can put it into your super.

This way, Vince feels, super can work as a form of painless saving.

Kate

Kate is 28, married and has been working as a caterer for 8 years. Three years ago she went out on her own and started a catering business which she is planning to expand with the help of a partner. Part of this expansion will be the hiring of employees.

> I'm going to need at least one or two people on full time so I will have to look in to paying super.
>
> I think it's good because it's for the future and it will take the pressure off the government having to pay everyone the pension.
>
> But I don't know if the employer should do it

> though. I think it should be optional like it used to be; I suppose I'm in the old world though.
>
> I suppose what we'll have to do is pay lower wages and put the rest into super as the contributions [determined by the Super Guarantee] go up. You can't keep expecting employers to dish out high wages and super, especially in a small business where the government hits you—with taxes and so on—like a tonne of bricks.

Regarding her own super, Kate thinks she has some floating around from one of her old jobs but she doesn't have an active super account at the moment. However, that will soon change.

> As a result of turning the business into a company, and with someone buying into it, we're going to have to split the funds. We're going to be paying off mortgages, or rents, or leases and with staff, we're not going to be drawing very high wages so we'll have to look into super too. What will happen is that we'll set it up so the company will pay us our super, that's what we're thinking of.

Kate feels that her first priority, however, is the success of her business.

> When you're a little company and you're just starting out, how do you know if it's going to work? It's just a gut instinct and you put all your money and effort into it. Super is a second thing and to me super is more a bonus at the end of the day.

Kate finds herself in the position well known to other small business owners of having to pay super and yet also having to think about being a recipient. Consequently she is in two minds as to whether it's a good thing. As she has said, we should all save more but she is not in love with the idea of employers having to pay it. With her business being the centre of her attention it's not surprising she is concerned about the expense of paying super to employees, however she is happy with the prospect of tax deductions.

> I think deductions are a good idea, of course I'd like to see more but at least it's something.

Jim

Jim is 26 and has worked as a storeman for the same employer since he was 18. He is more familiar with super than most as his boss has been paying him super for the last 6 years. Jim is very up front with his criticism of super.

> What about the people selling it to you. Every year they're taking something out then something more and

> something more and then you get statements and you're getting less than what you're thinking.
>
> When I was younger and working here I had money disappear on me so I went to see (the fund manager) and find out what was happening, no one was really there to tell me what it was all about.

Despite this, Jim thinks it's a good idea that everyone will have money waiting for them when they retire; however, he feels that super is not as important for him as it is for others because he plans to have plenty of assets.

> I've nearly paid my house off so with that it's OK for me because I've got other plans.
>
> I don't think I'll need to put my own money into super because when I retire, at 50 or whatever, I don't think I'll need a whole heap of money, just that super I've got from here, or wherever, and other money I've saved.

Jim classes himself as a 'saver'. He has nearly paid for his house in just over four years because he was able to scrape together a large deposit to put towards it. This was a habit he started when he was young.

> When I was at school I used to get two dollars a day from my mum for helping her clean a bank. By the time I got my licence I'd saved enough to buy a car.

While Jim saves to buy assets and not for his retirement, he points out that it's a bit different from the usual pattern of spending that most young people get into. He believes saving to buy a house and contributing to your super fulfils the same purpose. Whatever the type, Jim is of the opinion that saving is a good thing.

> When you get a job with half decent money, you just want to spend, spend, spend. And it's easy to do because everyone is doing it.

> Budgeting is the main thing; if you can budget then you're halfway there, but if you don't have a budget and you don't set yourself goals then you can easily blow it away.

Jim sees super as a means to help people to budget and save but thinks it will be more useful for the young as opposed to those who started receiving super later in life.

> By the time I retire it'll be fine and the people who are younger here [at work] and everywhere else—wherever they go they're going to get super.
> But people about 35 or 40 who haven't had it for that long aren't going to have as much.

Jim, like many others, has his suspicions about super but feels that the principle is a good one.

> It's a good idea to have money waiting for everyone when they retire, it's just how you do it that's the thing.

Jenny

Jenny is 19 years of age, has worked in a fast-food restaurant for four years, currently on a permanent casual basis, and she is studying Japanese at TAFE. She feels that at this point in her life there is no need to worry about retirement.

> I'm only 19, give me a break. It's just too far down the track to consider.

Jenny says she has no idea what super is about and whether she has any.

> It's just something which comes up on the pay cheque. They could say 'we're taking out such and such a week', but who knows what happens to the money?

And she doubts if she is alone wondering this.

I don't think a lot of people understand that it's going on. There should be more information around so they can find out.

However, Jenny concedes that investing money is not altogether a bad thing.

And thinking about it now, I suppose it is easier if someone invests the money for you, but you should have some sort of say—keep a record or whatever.

Jenny feels that the introduction of compulsory employee contributions will affect people in different ways, depending on their circumstances and how much it amounts to.

If they take out only small amounts each week, I'm sure it wouldn't really matter, but if it was a lot, it could create problems for everyone living out of home, renting their own place or whatever.

Jenny plans to go into the management training program offered by her employer but she isn't certain if she will be working with them in a few years time. She imagined that her super would automatically follow her to her next job. When told about the process of rolling over she is honest enough to admit to being confused. Jenny thought that if it were possible, more should be done to make the process a lot easier to do.

It doesn't sound like it can be simplified, but if that's possible it would be more beneficial I guess.

RESPONSE
. . . .

The varied backgrounds and occupations of these young people illustrate the point that super has an impact on just about all of us. Some of them were positive about super, others didn't think it was such a good idea, but nearly everyone recognised that super cannot be ignored. What is interesting, despite their different environments, is how often they voiced the same concerns and asked the same questions. The first part of the book deals with many of these, but we'll now look at some of these queries in brief and point you to the relevant part of the book if you want to read more.

I don't want to think about it now because I'm too young.

Too young to retire? Absolutely. Too young to think about super? Never.

Virtually everyone we talked to raised this doubt. At the centre of it is the thought that super only becomes relevant when you are coming up to retirement. The thing about super, and any form of saving for that matter, is that all the work is done ahead of time. Super is a reality long before retirement is, particularly since it is now compulsory.

This is not to say that we should all put extra money into our super accounts, that's up to you, but it is worthwhile to know what super is all about. (See Introduction and Why do I need super?, Chapter 2.)

The people running the super funds don't tell us enough about what's going on.

Again, just about everyone made this point. While many conceded it was up to them to find out about super, there was general agreement that super funds don't tell us enough about what happens to our money and how it all works.

Legislation brought in during 1993 requires super funds to inform their members about things such as administration costs and how the money has been invested. This should have led most funds to produce readily accessible information that is explained in simple terms if they weren't already. You should get information when you join and when you leave and every year you should receive a statement about your own account and the way the fund is performing.

There is a responsibility on your part, as a super fund member, to take the time to look through the material your fund sends you. If you feel that it is deficient in some way then you should take it up with the trustees.

Why are they performing so badly and is it safe?

Tony for one was not impressed with the return he was getting for his money and as a result he is not confident that super can deliver the retirement income he would want to have. Nerissa talked about money her parents lost on an investment they made and wondered if that could happen with her super.

There's no denying that super funds will have bad years when the fund's investment managers do not produce the returns they hoped for. However, there will be other years when the returns are better than expected. If you were saving for only one year this wouldn't give you comfort but super is a long-term savings plan.

Poor returns come with the territory when there is investment. But at the same time, the very risk which results in you making less money can also give your fund a better than expected result. (See What happens to my money?, Chapter 1 and Is my money safe?, Chapter 3.)

Are they charging too much?

Tony and Jim mentioned that their super has been eaten into by fees in the past while Superna was worried that withdrawing her super when she retires may involve paying hidden costs, since it happened to her father.

In 1995 the government brought in member protection legislation which requires funds to only draw their fees from the interest earned on accounts with less than $1000 in them. It's hoped that this will bring an end to the problem of small accounts being squashed under the excessive weight of fees.

With regard to hidden costs, and without knowing the details of the situation Superna's father found himself in, the rules of disclosure brought in during 1993 state that your fund must tell you everything about what you have to pay. The government is developing further disclosure requirements for agents. (See How much do I have to pay in fees? and How do I find out what fees I have to pay? in Chapter 3.)

How do I find out where all my super money is?

Kate, Chris, and Dani-lea talked about the difficulties of keeping track of their super money and the problems of having more than one super account open at the same time.

If you are trying to locate some super from an old job,

the first thing to do is to look through any literature which was sent to you concerning super. It may be that if you don't recognise one of the notices, it could be from the administrators of the fund your 'misplaced' super was paid into. Failing that you can get in contact with the people you worked for to find out which fund they paid super into. And finally, the Australian Tax Office from July 1996 will have a registry of lost super accounts, so if you contact them they might be able to help you out.

Having located your super you can then go about rolling it over into your current account. However, some funds may charge an exit fee to do so. So ask about this before you sign the forms. The lesson is to keep track of your super and roll it over, if necessary, as soon as possible. (See What do I do if I've lost my super?, Chapter 3.)

When can I get my hands on it?

Dani-lea mentioned that it would be nice to have at least some of her super money and just about everyone else made the point that retirement is too long to wait to get their money.

It's true that preservation rules generally require that your money stay in super until you retire and/or reach 65. However, there are occasions when super funds are released to a member, depending on the fund and as long as certain conditions are satisfied. They are:

- disability
- emigration
- financial hardship (determined by the Insurance and Superannuation Commission)
- early retirement (after the age of 55).

As you can see, a super fund, along with the Insurance and Superannuation Commission, will only release a member's funds ahead of time under certain circumstances. The reason it is so difficult to get access to your funds is because if you constantly dip into your super account there won't be much left when you have retired and need money to live on. (See Chapter 4.)

What will happen to the pension?

There were many comments during the course of the interviews to the effect that it will be difficult for the government to afford to pay the pension with our population ageing as significantly as it is. Dani-lea believed that there will be no age pension when she retires while Nerissa and Superna expressed concern that this could leave some people without much of an income during their retirement.

It is impossible to predict what will happen to the old age pension by the time this generation has retired, but there are certain trends developing which could still be having an effect in 40 years time.

The development of compulsory super is one of them. By raising the level of savings the current government hopes to relieve the pressure on social security. It has a plan to make workers contribute for their retirement and to provide a safety net pension. Currently the pension, at around a quarter of the average weekly wage, is means tested according to assets and income. It is possible that access to the pension will be more restricted in 40 years time. (See Will I get the pension?, Chapter 4.)

How much are they going to take out of my pay when the compulsory employee contributions come in?

Jenny wondered how much of her pay would be going towards her super when the employee contributions came through, and Vince felt it would be better if the employer takes it out of the pay before the employee receives it.

Here's how it will work. Starting in 1997/98, 1 per cent of your earnings as an employee will be contributed towards your super, which will rise to 2 per cent in 1998/99 before settling at 3 per cent in 1999/2000. This will be brought about by awards and enterprise bargains. If you are already contributing some of your salary to super, the changes will not affect you unless it is an amount less than these percentages.

However, most of you will benefit from the government's decision to match these contributions with its own payments. These will match your own contributions dollar for dollar as long as your income does not exceed 1.4 times the average wage. Currently that works out at $46 000 per year. It is then reduced by 5 cents for every dollar you earn over this amount which means the government contribution drops out when earnings reach $66 000 per year.

So the short answer is your employer will take out a dollar amount which depends on how much you earn and add it to the super that is contributed on your behalf as part of the Super Guarantee.

Do I have to pay it?

The point was made by both Chris and Superna that you should be able to choose whether you contribute your own money towards super, while Vince argued that it will be difficult to sell the idea of putting your own money away to people on low incomes.

Even though the government has not set compulsory employee contributions in legislation, it will be brought in by awards and enterprise bargains instead. In effect it should be no different than if it was part of the Super Guarantee legislation. Your employer will automatically take a certain percentage out of your pay and put it in with the rest of your super contributions. The reason it will start in 1997/98 and be phased in over three years is so that it will not have the drastic effect on your income as it would if 3 per cent was yanked out in one go.

Of course no one likes to have their pay reduced, even if it is going towards their retirement fund. Vince is right in saying it will be difficult to sell the idea of compulsory contributions to people. However, the offer of the government to match the compulsory amount with their own payments certainly sweetens the pot. Coupled with the phasing in of the employee payments, there should be little impact on workers, provided inflation is under control and awards and enterprise bargains are struck peacefully between unions and employer groups.

FOR MORE INFORMATION

About super in general

Insurance and Superannuation Commission

Phone: 13 10 60 (the cost of a local call Australia-wide)

Regarding complaints

The Superannuation Complaints Tribunal

Phone: 13 14 34 (the cost of a local call Australia-wide)

Regarding superannuation guarantee and lost benefits

The Australian Tax Office

Phone: 13 10 20 (the cost of a local call Australia-wide)

GLOSSARY

Accumulation A method of determining your benefit according to how much money has been contributed, what the return on investments has been, less the cost of fees and taxes.
Active Account One which is receiving contributions.
Annual Report A statement by the trustees to the fund members detailing the performance of the fund's investments in the past year, any developments in administration practices, as well as other titbits of information.
Assets Something you own which is worth money. An asset can be anything from a house to a stamp collection. In super they take the form of things like stocks, bonds and shares.
Beneficiary Nomination Form A form you fill out when you join a fund in which you nominate who will get your benefit if you die.
Benefit What you end up getting from your super when it is paid out.
Company Fund Fund started by an employer for the sole purpose of accepting superannuation contributions for employees of the company. They are usually offered by larger businesses.
Compound Interest This is interest which is paid on both the principal (i.e. the money you put in in the first

place) and the interest earned previously. This is how the benefit accumulates in most super funds.

Compulsory Employee Contribution The government intends to have all employees contributing 3 per cent of their after-tax earnings to their super from 1 July 1999. For those earning up to $66 000 a year the government will make matching contributions.

Contribution An amount of money paid into a person's super account.

Defined Benefit A method of determining your benefit which establishes it as a set amount. Usually this is worked out as a multiple of what your salary is just before retirement. However, it is not used often as most funds use an accumulation method to work out a member's benefit.

Diversification Spreading investments out so that the gains on one will balance, and hopefully outweigh, the losses on another.

Fees Various charges which amount to the cost of servicing your super account.

Fluctuation The rise and fall in the amount of your savings.

Fund Administrator A person or company that does the slog work, such as keeping records of accounts, answering inquiries and complaints, calculating benefits and so on.

Industry Fund Funds established by unions and employer groups which accept contributions for workers in a particular trade. Hospitality, retail, and construction are all industries which are represented by such a fund.

Insurance and Superannuation Commission A federal government body given the job of regulating the superannuation and insurance industries.

Investment Manager A person or company that takes

charge of investing the money in a super fund according to the guidelines of the investment strategy.

Investment Strategy The way the money in a super fund is invested. It is done according to a plan agreed by the trustees which refers to what type of investment the money will be put towards, the expected return, and the allowable risks.

Lump Sum All of your benefit paid to you in one go.

Member Someone who has an account in a fund. In other words, the punter (i.e. you and me).

Member Investment Choice Some funds offer their members a range of investment strategies. If you're a member of such a fund, you can choose what type of investments you want made on your behalf. Generally the choices on offer vary in rate of return and how much risk is involved.

Member Protection New legislation which protects small accounts from being eaten away by fees. Super funds are not allowed to charge members for fees in excess of what their money is earning if there is less than $1000 in the account.

Pension A type of payment. With regards to super and retirement income there are two varieties. That which is paid by social security and that which is regular income from super investments. However, they are both paid in the same amount each time and at regular intervals which is what makes them pensions.

Personal Fund Super that is established by and on behalf of an individual.

Preservation Regulation requires that, with a few exceptions (detailed in Chapter 4, When do I get my money?), your money must remain in super until you reach 65 years of age.

Public Offer Funds Set up by banks and insurance companies, public offer funds largely provide super for the self-employed and those who have a personal fund. They are not linked to a company or an industry.

Public Sector Fund Established by acts of parliament, these funds accept super contributions for government employees.

Reasonable Benefit Limit (RBL) Is the maximum amount of money you can receive from your super that is taxed at the concessional rate.

Return What your money makes after it's invested.

Superannuation A savings plan designed to provide income during retirement.

Superannuation Complaints Tribunal The body established to hear complaints against a decision made by the trustees of a fund.

Superannuation Guarantee Charge (Super Guarantee) The Superannuation Guarantee Charge requires an employer to contribute to their employees' super. As of 1 July 1995 it stands at 5 per cent of an employee's pay if the company pays less than 1 million on wages and 6 per cent if they pay more than 1 million. This will rise to be 9 per cent on 1 July 2002.

Superannuation Holding Account Reserve Scheme started by the Australian Tax Office to accept and hold contributions for us punters when the balance is less than $1200. It is designed to assist employers who do not have a fund to pay their employees' super into and to complement the member protection rules.

Transfer Protocol An industry program designed to make the process of moving super from fund to fund a bit easier.

Trust Deed The rule book for the operation of the fund which is legally binding. It sets out the terms on who can be appointed to manage the fund, how the money should be invested, how benefits will be paid, and so on.

Trustees People responsible for the management of a super fund and the conduct of its business by administrators and investment managers.

Vest When a member has his or her super 'vested' it means that the money is theirs. Sometimes a company pays super above the compulsory Super Guarantee amount and part or all of the balance has been held in reserve (usually 5 to 10 years) before it is vested to the employee. This is used to reward long-serving staff.

Everyone's Guide to Superannuation
Edna Carew and John Hoffmann

Sweeping changes to the nation's superannuation system have transformed the retirement outlook for everyone. Every Australian in receipt of a wage or salary now contributes to his or her own future by way of investing in superannuation funds. This means that we all have a relatively painless way of creating substantial savings for use after retirement from the workforce—when those savings will be most useful.

But, to many people, superannuation remains a worrying mystery. This book, by finance writers widely applauded for their ability to explain complex financial ideas simply and accurately, will enable you to understand the opportunities superannuation presents—opportunities to create a better financial future.

1 86448 031 9

Managing Superannuation
A Trustee's Guide

New superannuation legislation has created a new class of money managers: the representatives of employees who, as superannuation fund trustees, are responsible for the prudent investment of tens of millions of dollars of their fellow employees' compulsory and discretionary contributions.

Managing Superannuation is a book for all trustees including those who represent employers. It explains what trustees legal duties and responsibilities are, and how they can carry them out as efficiently as possible.

ASFA, the association that represents superannuation plans throughout Australia, has produced *Managing Superannuation* for three reasons:

- **to describe in plain language the role of trustees and their duties**
- **to stimulate thinking and discussion about the role of trustees**
- **to encourage people to put themselves forward to act as trustees of superannuation plans.**

While anyone interested in superannuation will find this book useful, it has been specifically written for:

- **new trustees**—to help them to understand their duties and responsibilities
- **seasoned trustees**—as a 'refresher course'
- **advisers and those who act for trustees**—to help them understand more clearly how they fit into running superannuation plans.

1 86373 970 X